YouTube Animation for Everyone - Create and Grow Your Channel

Sualeha Bhatti

TABLE OF CONTENTS

INTRODUCTION

Who Is This Book For?

In the rapidly evolving world of digital content, video has emerged as a dominant force. With platforms like YouTube, Instagram, TikTok, and Facebook, there's an insatiable appetite for fresh, engaging content. But standing out in this crowded space is no easy task. That's where animated videos come in.

This book is designed for anyone who dreams of harnessing the power of animation to increase their social media presence or generate passive income. Whether you're a complete beginner curious about animation, a small business owner looking to create unique content, or an aspiring YouTuber wanting to make a mark with something different—this book is for you.

You may be a social media enthusiast who's already dabbled in video creation but wants to elevate your content with animation. Perhaps you're a professional looking to diversify your skills, or maybe you're a creative soul who's been searching for a way to turn your passion into profit. Regardless of your background, if you're excited about the potential of animated videos, this book will guide you from concept to creation and beyond.

Why Animated Videos?

Animated videos have a unique appeal. They can simplify complex ideas, tell captivating stories, and evoke emotions in ways that live-action videos often cannot. With animation, the only limit is your imagination. You can create entire worlds, bring characters to life, and convey messages with a distinct style that's truly your own.

Moreover, animated videos are incredibly versatile. They can be used for educational content, explainer videos, advertisements, entertainment, and so much more. The popularity of animated content is on the rise, and audiences love the creativity and innovation that these videos bring to their screens.

But beyond creativity, there's a practical side to animation as well. Animated videos tend to have higher engagement rates, better retention, and are often more shareable than other types of content. They allow you to stand out in a sea of similar videos, giving you a unique edge on platforms like YouTube.

Understanding the Potential: Passive Income & Social Media Growth

Creating animated videos isn't just about being creative; it's about tapping into the potential for passive income and significant social media growth. YouTube, in particular, offers a myriad of monetization opportunities—from ad revenue to sponsored content, affiliate marketing, and even merchandise sales. By building a library of engaging animated content, you can create a steady stream of income that grows over time.

Social media presence is another powerful byproduct of animated content. High-quality animations can go viral, bringing a surge of new subscribers and followers to your channel or profile. With consistent effort and strategic content creation, you can build a loyal audience that not only engages with your videos but also supports your growth as a content creator.

This book will show you how to turn your creative ideas into profitable content. You'll learn how to plan, create, and promote animated videos that resonate with your audience and help you achieve your goals—whether that's growing a successful YouTube channel, building a brand, or simply enjoying the rewards of your hard work.

CHAPTER 1: GETTING STARTED WITH ANIMATED VIDEOS

Understanding the Basics of Animation

Animation is the art of bringing still images to life. It's a powerful medium that allows creators to tell stories, explain concepts, and engage audiences in a way that live-action video often cannot. But before diving into the creation process, it's important to understand what animation really is and how it works.

At its core, animation involves the rapid display of a sequence of images that differ slightly from one another. When these images are shown in quick succession, they create the illusion of movement. This is the principle behind all animation, whether it's traditional hand-drawn cartoons, modern 3D animations, or even simple GIFs.

Animations can range from simple and minimalistic to complex and highly detailed. The level of detail, the type of animation, and the tools you use will all depend on your goals, your audience, and your resources. Whether you're looking to create short, catchy animations for social media or full-length animated stories for YouTube, understanding the basics is the first step in your journey.

Types of Animated Videos

Animation comes in many forms, each with its own unique style and applications. Here are some of the most popular types of animation you might consider for your content:

1. **2D Animation**: This is the traditional form of animation where characters and scenes are created in a two-dimensional space. Think of classic cartoons like "The Simpsons" or "Looney Tunes." 2D animation is great for storytelling and is often easier to learn for beginners. Tools like Adobe Animate or Toon Boom are popular for creating 2D animations.

2. **3D Animation**: In 3D animation, characters and objects are created

in a three-dimensional space, giving them depth and realism. This type of animation is used in movies, video games, and more complex animations. 3D animation requires more advanced skills and tools, like Blender or Maya, but it offers a level of realism that 2D cannot.

3. **Stop-Motion Animation**: This technique involves physically manipulating objects and taking a series of photographs to create movement. Think of classics like "Wallace & Gromit" or "The Nightmare Before Christmas." While stop-motion can be time-consuming, it offers a unique and tactile quality that's hard to replicate with digital animation.

4. **Motion Graphics**: Often used in explainer videos, motion graphics involve animating text, shapes, and other design elements to communicate a message. This style is great for creating dynamic presentations or infographics and is commonly used in marketing videos.

5. **Whiteboard Animation**: A type of animation where drawings are created on a whiteboard (or simulated digitally) to tell a story or explain a concept. It's a popular choice for educational content and explainer videos due to its simplicity and clarity.

Each of these types of animation has its strengths and is suited for different types of content. As you explore these styles, consider what fits best with your brand, your audience, and the message you want to convey.

Choosing the Right Type of Animation for Your Channel

Selecting the appropriate type of animation for your channel is a crucial decision that will shape the look, feel, and overall impact of your content. Here are some key factors to consider when choosing the right animation style:

1. **Your Target Audience**: Understanding your audience is the first step in choosing the right animation style. For instance, if your target audience is children, colorful and playful 2D animations might be the most effective. On the other hand, a more professional audience might respond better to clean, polished motion graphics.

2. **Your Content Goals**: Consider what you aim to achieve with your videos. If your goal is to explain complex ideas in an easy-to-digest format, motion graphics or whiteboard animations might be your best bet. For storytelling or creating a more immersive experience,

2D or 3D animations could be more effective.

3. **Your Skill Level and Resources**: Your current skills and the tools you have access to will also influence your decision. If you're new to animation, starting with a simpler style like 2D or white board animation might be a smart move. As you gain more experience, you can explore more complex forms like 3D or stop-motion animation.

4. **Your Budget**: Different animation styles require different levels of investment in terms of time, software, and sometimes hardware. 3D animation, for instance, often requires more powerful computers and expensive software, whereas 2D animation can be done on a more modest setup.

5. **Your Brand Identity**: The animation style you choose should align with your overall brand identity. For example, if your brand is fun and whimsical, a vibrant 2D animation might be a perfect fit. If your brand is more serious and professional, sleek motion graphics might be more appropriate.

By taking these factors into account, you can select an animation style that not only aligns with your goals and resources but also resonates with your target audience. The right choice will help you create content that stands out and effectively communicates your message, ultimately driving growth and engagement for your channel.

CHAPTER 2: PLANNING YOUR ANIMATED VIDEO CONTENT

Effective planning is the cornerstone of successful animated videos. Whether you're creating content for YouTube, Instagram, or another social media platform, having a clear plan will help you stay organized, focused, and on track to achieve your goals. This chapter will guide you through the essential steps of planning your animated video content, from identifying your niche to creating a production schedule that ensures consistent, high-quality output.

Identifying Your Niche

Before you start creating animated videos, it's crucial to identify your niche— the specific area or topic that your content will focus on. Your niche defines your brand, shapes your content, and helps you connect with a particular audience. Choosing the right niche is a key factor in building a successful online presence.

1. **Assess Your Interests and Expertise**: Start by considering what you're passionate about and knowledgeable in. What topics do you enjoy discussing or learning about? What skills or expertise do you have that could be valuable to others? Your niche should align with your interests and strengths so that you can create content that is both engaging and authentic.

2. **Research Your Audience**: Understanding your target audience is essential for selecting a niche that will resonate with them. Who are the people you want to reach with your videos? What are their interests, needs, and challenges? Conducting audience research— through surveys, social media, and competitor analysis—can help you identify gaps in the market that your content can fill.

3. **Analyze the Competition**: Take a look at other creators in your potential niche. What type of content are they producing? How successful are they? Analyzing the competition can help you identify opportunities to differentiate your content and offer something unique. Look for ways to provide a fresh perspective or explore sub-niches that are less saturated.

4

4.   **Define Your Unique Selling Proposition (USP)**: Your USP is what sets you apart from other creators in your niche. It could be your unique style of animation, a specific approach to storytelling, or a particular theme that runs through your content. Defining your USP will help you attract and retain a loyal audience.

By carefully selecting your niche, you can focus your efforts on creating content that speaks directly to a specific audience, making it easier to grow your channel and build a strong, engaged community.

Developing a Content Strategy

Once you've identified your niche, the next step is to develop a content strategy. Your content strategy is your roadmap for creating and distributing videos that align with your goals and resonate with your audience. It outlines the type of content you'll produce, how often you'll post, and how you'll engage with your viewers.

1. **Set Clear Goals**: What do you want to achieve with your animated videos? Whether your goals include increasing your subscriber count, generating passive income, or building brand awareness, having clear, measurable objectives will guide your content creation process.

2. **Define Your Content Pillars**: Content pillars are the main topics or themes that your videos will focus on. For example, if your niche is educational content, your pillars might include tutorials, explainer videos, and interviews with experts. These pillars will form the foundation of your content strategy, ensuring that your videos are consistent and aligned with your brand.

3. **Create a Content Calendar**: Consistency is key to building a successful online presence. A content calendar helps you plan and schedule your videos in advance, so you always have fresh content ready to publish. Your calendar should include the video topic, the type of animation, the script or storyboard deadline, and the planned publication date.

4.   **Engage with Your Audience**: A successful content strategy isn't just about creating videos; it's also about engaging with your audience. Respond to comments, ask for feedback, and use social media to interact with your viewers. This engagement will help you build a loyal community and gain insights into what your audience wants to see more of.

5. **Monitor and Adjust**: Your content strategy should be flexible and adaptable. Monitor the performance of your videos using analytics tools like YouTube Analytics or social media insights. Pay attention to which types of content perform best and adjust your strategy accordingly. This data-driven approach will help you refine your content and maximize your results over time.

With a well-defined content strategy, you'll have a clear direction for your animated videos, making it easier to stay consistent, engage your audience, and achieve your goals.

Scripting and Storyboarding

Great animation starts with a great script. Your script is the blueprint for your video, outlining the dialogue, actions, and scenes that will bring your story to life. Once your script is in place, storyboarding helps you visualize how your video will unfold, scene by scene.

1. **Writing the Script**:
   - *Start with an Outline*: Begin by outlining the key points or messages you want to convey in your video. This outline will serve as the backbone of your script, ensuring that your content is structured and focused.
   - *Craft Engaging Dialogue*: If your video includes characters or a narrator, spend time crafting dialogue that is natural, engaging, and aligned with your brand voice. Keep in mind the pacing of your animation—dialogue should match the timing and flow of your visuals.
   - *Include Visual Cues*: In addition to dialogue, your script should include visual cues that describe what the audience will see on screen. These cues will guide the animation process and ensure that the visuals align with the narrative.
   - *Keep It Concise*: Attention spans are short, especially on social media. Aim to keep your script concise and to the point, avoiding unnecessary details or long-winded explanations.

2. **Creating the Storyboard**:
   - *Visualize Each Scene*: A storyboard is a sequence of sketches or images that represent each scene of your video. It helps you plan the visual flow of your story, ensuring that each scene transitions smoothly into the next.
   - *Define Key Frames*: Key frames are the most important

moments in your animation—where significant actions or changes occur. Identify these key frames in your storyboard to highlight crucial points in your narrative.

- *Plan Camera Angles and Movements*: Storyboarding is also an opportunity to plan the camera angles and movements for your animation. Consider how close-ups, wide shots, and camera pans can enhance the storytelling.
- *Annotate with Notes*: Include notes alongside your storyboard sketches to clarify details like timing, transitions, and any special effects you plan to use. These annotations will serve as a guide during the animation process.

A well-written script and detailed storyboard are essential tools for bringing your animated video to life. They ensure that your story is clear, your visuals are aligned with your narrative, and your animation process is efficient and organized.

Character and Scene Design

Designing characters and scenes is one of the most creative and enjoyable aspects of animation. Your characters are the heart of your story, and the scenes they inhabit set the tone and atmosphere of your video.

1. **Character Design**:
   - *Define Character Traits*: Start by defining the traits, personalities, and roles of your characters. Are they serious, playful, quirky, or authoritative? These traits will influence their appearance, behavior, and how they interact with other characters.
   - *Sketch Initial Concepts*: Begin with rough sketches to explore different looks and styles for your characters. Experiment with different shapes, proportions, and features until you find a design that fits your narrative and brand.
   - *Choose Colors and Details*: Color plays a significant role in character design, conveying mood and personality. Choose a color palette that aligns with your brand and enhances the character's traits. Pay attention to details like clothing, accessories, and facial expressions, as these will add depth to your characters.
   - *Create Turnarounds and Expressions*: A character turnaround is a series of drawings that show the character from multiple angles (front, side, back). Create turnarounds and expression sheets to ensure consistency in your

animation, especially if you're working with a team.

2. **Scene Design:**
   - *Establish the Setting*: The setting of your scenes should complement the story and characters. Consider the environment where the action takes place—whether it's a bustling city, a serene forest, or a futuristic world. The setting should reflect the tone and theme of your video.
   - *Design Backgrounds*: Backgrounds are more than just scenery; they contribute to the mood and atmosphere of your animation. Design backgrounds that are visually appealing but not too distracting, allowing your characters to stand out.
   - *Plan for Depth and Movement*: If you're creating a 3D animation or using parallax effects in 2D, plan for depth and movement in your scenes. Layering elements and incorporating perspective will give your scenes a sense of realism and dynamism.
   - *Consider Lighting and Color Schemes*: Lighting and color schemes play a crucial role in setting the mood of your scenes. Consider how different lighting conditions (e.g., bright daylight, moody twilight) and color schemes (e.g., warm vs. cool tones) can enhance the storytelling.

Character and scene design are integral to creating a compelling animated video. Thoughtful design choices will bring your story to life and engage your audience on a deeper level.

Creating a Video Production Schedule

Animation can be a time-consuming process, especially if you're working on a complex project. Creating a video production schedule will help you manage your time effectively, stay organized, and ensure that your videos are completed on time and to a high standard.

1. **Break Down the Process**: Start by breaking down the animation process into smaller, manageable tasks. These tasks might include scripting, storyboarding, character design, background design, animating, editing, and post-production.

2. **Set Milestones and Deadlines**: Assign deadlines to each task and set milestones to track your progress. For example, you might set a milestone for completing the script, another for finishing the storyboard, and so on. Milestones will help you stay on track and make sure you're meeting your overall production timeline.

3. **Allocate Resources**: Determine what resources (e.g., time, software, equipment) you'll need for each task. If you're working with a team, assign specific tasks to team members based on their skills and expertise. Make sure everyone understands their responsibilities and deadlines.

4. **Plan for Revisions**: Revisions are a natural part of the animation process, so be sure to build time for revisions into your schedule. Whether it's adjusting the script, refining the animation, or making changes based on feedback, planning for revisions will help you avoid last-minute stress.

5. **Stay Flexible**: While it's important to have a schedule, it's also important to stay flexible. Unexpected challenges can arise during the animation process, so be prepared to adjust your schedule as needed. Staying adaptable will help you maintain a positive workflow and deliver high-quality results.

By creating a detailed video production schedule, you'll be able to manage your time and resources effectively, stay on top of your tasks, and deliver animated videos that meet your goals and deadlines.

CHAPTER 3: TOOLS AND SOFTWARE FOR ANIMATION

Creating animated videos might sound like a complex task reserved for professional graphic designers, but the truth is, anyone can do it with the right tools and a bit of guidance. Whether you're a student looking to share your creative ideas, a housewife interested in starting a YouTube channel, or simply someone who wants to increase their social media presence, this chapter will introduce you to easy-to-use tools and software that can help you create engaging animated videos without needing a background in graphic design.

Overview of Popular Animation Software

When it comes to creating animations, you don't need to be a tech wizard. There are plenty of user-friendly tools that make it easy for anyone to create fun and professional-looking videos. Here's an overview of some of the most popular options:

1. **Animaker:**
   - *Type*: Web-based 2D Animation
   - *Best For*: Beginners looking to create explainer videos, social media content, or simple animations.
   - *Overview*: Animaker is a drag-and-drop animation tool that runs directly in your web browser. It comes with pre-built templates, characters, and scenes that make it easy to put together a video in minutes. Whether you want to create a quick explainer video, a fun social media post, or an animated birthday message, Animaker is a great place to start.

2. **Canva:**
   - *Type*: Web-based Design Tool with Animation Features
   - *Best For*: Creating animated social media posts, presentations, and simple videos.
   - *Overview*: Canva is widely known for its easy-to-use design features, but it also allows you to create simple animations. You can animate text, images, and other elements with just a few clicks. Canva is perfect for anyone who wants to add a bit of movement to their social media graphics or create

short, engaging videos without diving into full-fledged animation software.

3. **Powtoon**:
   - *Type*: Web-based Animation Tool
   - *Best For*: Creating animated presentations, explainer videos, and marketing content.
   - *Overview*: Powtoon is another web-based tool that simplifies the animation process. It offers a variety of templates, characters, and scenes, allowing you to create professional-looking animations with little effort. Powtoon is especially useful for creating engaging presentations or marketing videos, making it a good choice if you want to stand out on platforms like YouTube or LinkedIn.

4. **Doodly**:
   - *Type*: Whiteboard Animation Software
   - *Best For*: Creating whiteboard explainer videos.
   - *Overview*: Doodly lets you create whiteboard-style animations, where a hand draws images and text on the screen as you narrate. It's incredibly simple to use and perfect for making educational content, tutorials, or any video where you want to explain something in a clear and engaging way.

5. **Krita**:
   - *Type*: Free 2D Animation Software
   - *Best For*: Those interested in hand-drawn animations or more detailed 2D work.
   - *Overview*: Krita is a free, open-source software primarily known for digital painting, but it also includes animation features. While it's a bit more advanced than some of the other tools mentioned, it's still accessible and comes with plenty of tutorials to help you get started.

Free vs. Paid Tools

One of the first decisions you'll need to make when choosing animation software is whether to go with free or paid tools. Both have their benefits, and the right choice depends on your needs, budget, and goals.

1. **Free Tools**:
   - *Krita*: A powerful free tool that's great for 2D animation if you're willing to spend some time learning how to use it.

- *Canva*: Free to use, with additional paid features available. Great for creating simple animated posts and videos without any design experience.

- *Powtoon* (Free Version): Offers basic features for creating animated videos. The free version has some limitations, such as watermarked exports and limited templates, but it's enough to get started.

2. **Pros of Free Tools**:
   - No financial investment required
   - Good for experimenting and learning the basics
   - Many offer community support and tutorials

3. **Cons of Free Tools**:
   - Limited features compared to paid versions
   - Some may have watermarks or other restrictions
   - Less professional support or fewer updates

4. **Paid Tools**:
   - *Animaker*: Offers a free version, but the paid plans unlock more templates, higher quality exports, and additional features.
   - *Powtoon* (Paid Version): Removes watermarks, offers higher quality exports, and gives access to more templates and features.
   - *Doodly*: A paid tool that's very user-friendly and perfect for creating whiteboard animations.

5. **Pros of Paid Tools**:
   - Access to more advanced features
   - No watermarks or limitations on exports
   - Better support and regular updates
   -

6. **Cons of Paid Tools**:
   - Requires an upfront investment or subscription fee
   - Can be more complex, with features you may not need if you're just starting out

Beginner-Friendly Options

If you're new to animation and don't want to feel overwhelmed, starting with beginner-friendly software can make a big difference. These tools are designed to be intuitive and easy to use, even if you have no prior experience.

1. **Animaker**:
   - *Why It's Beginner-Friendly*: Animaker's drag-and-drop interface and pre-built templates make it easy for anyone to create animated videos without needing to learn complex software. You can pick a template, customize it with your text and images, and have a video ready to share in minutes.

2. **Canva**:
   - *Why It's Beginner-Friendly*: Canva's animation features are very basic and easy to use. You simply choose an element (like text or an image) and apply a simple animation effect. It's perfect for creating animated social media posts, intros for videos, or simple presentations.

3. **Powtoon**:
   - *Why It's Beginner-Friendly*: Powtoon is designed for non-designers. Its user-friendly interface and ready-made templates mean you can create polished, animated videos without needing any animation experience. It's ideal for those who want to create engaging content quickly.

4. **Doodly**:
   - *Why It's Beginner-Friendly*: Doodly is straightforward, with a focus on creating whiteboard animations. The process involves selecting images and text, arranging them on a timeline, and letting the software do the rest. It's especially good for educational videos or tutorials where explaining concepts visually is key.

Additional Tools for Editing and Post-Production

After creating your animation, you might want to edit the video, add music, or include some sound effects. Here are some easy-to-use tools that can help you polish your final product:

1. **InShot**:
   - *Best For*: Video editing on mobile devices.
   - *Overview*: InShot is a mobile app that makes video editing simple. You can trim clips, add music, apply filters, and even include text and stickers. It's great for editing your animated videos before sharing them on social media platforms like

Instagram or TikTok.

2. **Kapwing**:
   - *Best For*: Web-based video editing.
   - *Overview*: Kapwing is an online video editor that's perfect for quick edits. You can upload your animation, trim it, add subtitles, and include music or sound effects. It's user-friendly and doesn't require any software downloads, making it a convenient choice for beginners.

3. **Audacity**:
   - *Best For*: Audio editing and recording.
   - *Overview*: Audacity is a free, easy-to-use audio editing software that's perfect for recording voiceovers or editing audio tracks for your animations. It's a great tool for improving the sound quality of your videos and adding professional touches like background music or sound effects.

4. **iMovie**:
   - *Best For*: Video editing on Mac devices.
   - *Overview*: iMovie comes free with Mac devices and is an excellent option for basic video editing. It offers a range of features for trimming clips, adding transitions, and including music. It's user-friendly and works well for creating polished videos ready for YouTube or other platforms.

Selecting the Right Tools for Your Budget and Skills

Choosing the right tools depends on what you want to achieve with your animations, how much you're willing to spend, and how comfortable you are with learning new software. Here's how to pick the best tools for your needs:

1. **Start with Free Tools**: If you're just starting out and don't want to invest money right away, begin with free tools like Canva, Krita, or the free versions of Animaker or Powtoon. These will help you get a feel for animation without any financial commitment.

2. **Consider Your Goals**: Think about what you want to do with your animations. Are you looking to create simple social media posts, or are you aiming to build a YouTube channel with more polished videos? Your goals will help determine whether you need more advanced (and potentially paid) tools.

3. **Look for Ease of Use**: Choose software that matches your comfort level. If you're not tech-savvy, opt for tools that offer drag-and-drop

functionality and plenty of templates, like Animaker or Canva. As you gain more experience, you can explore more advanced options if needed.

4. **Budget Wisely**: If you decide to invest in paid tools, start with the basics and upgrade only when you feel comfortable. Many tools offer monthly subscriptions, so you can try them out without committing to a full year upfront.

By starting with user-friendly tools and gradually exploring more advanced options, you can create engaging animated videos that enhance your social media presence or grow your YouTube channel—no graphic design experience required.

CHAPTER 4: BRINGING YOUR CHARACTERS AND STORIES TO LIFE

Now that you've selected the tools you'll use to create your animations, it's time to dive into the fun part: bringing your characters and stories to life. This chapter will guide you through the basics of character design, animating your creations, incorporating sound and music, and using voiceovers effectively. We'll also cover best practices for making your animations as engaging and impactful as possible.

Character Design Basics

Your characters are the heart of your animation. They are the ones who will tell your story, connect with your audience, and make your content memorable. But don't worry—designing characters doesn't require you to be a professional artist. Here are some simple tips to get started:

1. **Keep It Simple**: Especially if you're new to animation, start with simple character designs. Think about classic cartoon characters like the ones you see in children's books—big eyes, basic shapes, and bold colors. Simple designs are not only easier to animate, but they're also more likely to be visually appealing and memorable.

2. **Focus on Personality**: Your character's personality should shine through in their design. Is your character cheerful and friendly, or are they serious and focused? Use shapes, colors, and expressions to reflect these traits. For example, round shapes and warm colors often suggest a friendly and approachable character, while sharp angles and cool colors might suggest a more serious or reserved personality.

3. **Use Inspiration**: Look at other animations, cartoons, and even everyday objects for inspiration. What do you like about their designs? How do they use color and shape to convey personality? Don't hesitate to mix and match ideas to create something uniquely yours.

4. **Test Different Expressions**: Draw or create different facial expressions for your character—happy, sad, surprised, angry, etc.

This will help you get a feel for how your character will look in various situations and make your animation more dynamic.

5. **Create a Character Sheet**: A character sheet is a simple document where you sketch your character from different angles (front, side, back) and include a few key expressions. This will serve as a reference when you start animating, ensuring your character looks consistent throughout your video.

Animating Characters and Objects

Once your characters are designed, it's time to bring them to life with animation. Whether you're using simple software or something more advanced, these basic principles will help you create smooth and engaging animations:

1. **Start with Basic Movements**: Begin by animating simple actions like walking, waving, or turning their head. These basic movements are the building blocks of animation and will help you get comfortable with the process.

2. **Use Keyframes**: In animation, keyframes are the start and end points of a movement. For example, if your character is raising their hand, you'll create a keyframe with the hand down and another with the hand up. The software will then fill in the in-between frames, creating the illusion of movement.

3. **Pay Attention to Timing**: The timing of your animation affects how realistic and engaging it looks. Faster movements can convey excitement or urgency, while slower movements can suggest calmness or hesitation. Play around with the speed of different actions to see what works best for your story.

4. **Animate Objects, Too**: Don't forget to animate the objects around your characters. Whether it's a bouncing ball, a door opening, or leaves rustling in the wind, animating objects adds depth to your scenes and makes your world feel more alive.

5. **Practice, Practice, Practice**: Animation is a skill that improves with practice. Start with short, simple animations and gradually work your way up to more complex scenes as you gain confidence.

Incorporating Sound and Music

Sound and music play a crucial role in setting the mood and enhancing the impact of your animation. Here's how to effectively incorporate audio into your videos:

1. **Choose the Right Background Music**: Music sets the tone for your animation, so choose a track that matches the mood of your story. For example, light, upbeat music works well for fun, playful scenes, while a slower, more dramatic track might be better for serious moments. Websites like YouTube's Audio Library, Free Music Archive, and Epidemic Sound offer a wide range of royalty-free music that you can use in your videos.

2. **Add Sound Effects**: Sound effects make your animations more immersive. Whether it's footsteps, birds chirping, or doors creaking, adding these sounds helps bring your scenes to life. You can find free sound effects online or use the ones provided in your animation software.

3. **Balance the Audio**: Make sure your background music and sound effects don't overpower each other or your voiceover. Adjust the volume levels so that each element is clear and easy to hear. Many video editing tools, like InShot or Kapwing, allow you to easily control audio levels.

4. **Use Silence Effectively**: Sometimes, silence can be just as powerful as sound. Don't be afraid to include moments of quiet in your animation, especially if you want to build tension or draw attention to a particular scene.

Voiceover Tips and Techniques

Adding a voiceover to your animation can help you connect with your audience and convey your message more effectively. Here's how to get started:

1. **Write a Script**: Before recording your voiceover, write a script that clearly outlines what you want to say. Keep it simple and direct—remember, your voiceover should complement your visuals, not overwhelm them.

2. **Practice Your Delivery**: Read your script out loud a few times before recording. Pay attention to your tone, pace, and pronunciation. Try to sound natural and engaging, as if you're speaking directly to your audience.

3. **Use a Good Microphone**: You don't need a professional studio setup, but using a decent microphone will make a big difference in the quality of your voiceover. If you don't have a dedicated microphone, even the one on your smartphone can work if you record in a quiet environment.

4. **Record in a Quiet Space**: Find a quiet place to record your voiceover, free from background noise and distractions. If possible, use a room with soft furnishings (like carpets or curtains) to reduce echo.

5. **Edit Your Recording**: Use a simple audio editing tool like Audacity to clean up your recording. You can remove background noise, cut out mistakes, and adjust the volume. Don't forget to listen back to the final version to make sure it sounds clear and professional.

Best Practices for Engaging Animations

Finally, here are some best practices to keep in mind to ensure your animations are as engaging and effective as possible:

1. **Tell a Story**: Even if your animation is short, try to include a clear beginning, middle, and end. Storytelling is a powerful way to connect with your audience and make your content more memorable.

2. **Keep It Short and Sweet**: Attention spans on social media can be short, so aim to keep your animations concise. Focus on delivering your message quickly and clearly, without unnecessary details.

3. **Use Color and Contrast**: Bold colors and strong contrasts can help your characters and scenes stand out. However, be mindful of your color choices and make sure they're consistent with the mood and tone of your story.

4. **Engage with Your Audience**: Ask questions, encourage comments, or include a call-to-action at the end of your video. Engaging with your audience helps build a community around your content and encourages viewers to share your videos with others.

5. **Be Consistent**: Whether it's your character design, animation style, or posting schedule, consistency helps build your brand and keeps your audience coming back for more.

By following these tips and techniques, you'll be able to create animations that not only look great but also captivate your audience and help you grow your social media presence or YouTube channel.

CHAPTER 5: EDITING AND POST-PRODUCTION

Creating the animation is just one part of the process. The magic really comes together in the editing and post-production phase, where you refine your work, add special touches, and prepare your video for sharing with the world. In this chapter, we'll cover the basics of video editing, how to add special effects and transitions, ways to optimize your video quality for different platforms, and how to finalize your video for upload.

Video Editing Basics

Editing is where your animation starts to take its final shape. Even if your animation is simple, a bit of editing can make it more polished and professional. Here's how to get started with video editing:

1. **Import Your Animation**: The first step is to import your animation into a video editing software. If you've used a tool like Animaker or Canva, you might be able to export your animation directly into a video file. For editing, popular tools include iMovie (for Mac users), Windows Video Editor, InShot (for mobile editing), and Kapwing (a web-based editor).

2. **Trim and Cut**: Once your animation is in the editor, you can trim any unnecessary parts and cut out sections that don't add to your story. This helps keep your video concise and engaging. For example, you might remove a long pause or cut down on repeated actions to maintain a good flow.

3. **Arrange Your Clips**: If you have multiple scenes or animation clips, arrange them in the right order on your timeline. Make sure the transitions between scenes are smooth. Rearranging clips can also help improve the pacing of your video, making it more dynamic.

4. **Adjust the Timing**: Timing is crucial in animation. Use your editing tool to adjust the timing of scenes or actions. If a movement feels too fast or too slow, you can tweak the duration to make it feel more natural and effective.

5. **Add Text and Titles**: Most editing tools allow you to add text to your video. This can be useful for introducing your video, adding captions, or including calls-to-action like "Subscribe" or "Follow." Make sure

the text is easy to read and doesn't clutter the screen.

Adding Special Effects and Transitions

Special effects and transitions can enhance your video, making it more visually appealing and engaging. Here's how to use them effectively:

1. **Simple Transitions**: Transitions help you move smoothly from one scene to another. Basic transitions like fades, wipes, or slides are easy to apply and add a professional touch to your video. However, avoid overusing flashy transitions—they can be distracting and take away from the content.

2. **Visual Effects**: Depending on your editing software, you might have access to visual effects like blurs, color filters, or motion effects. These can be used to emphasize certain parts of your animation, create mood, or add a unique style. For example, adding a slight blur to the background can make your characters stand out more.

3. **Sound Effects**: Adding sound effects during editing can bring your animation to life. Whether it's the sound of footsteps, a door creaking, or birds chirping, well-placed sound effects enhance the realism of your video. Be careful not to overdo it—too many sound effects can be overwhelming.

4. **Music and Voiceover**: If you haven't added background music or voiceover during the animation phase, now is the time to do it. Make sure your music complements the mood of the animation and that the voiceover is clear and well-timed with the visuals.

Optimizing Video Quality for Different Platforms

Once your video is edited and looks great, it's important to optimize it for the platforms where you'll be sharing it. Different platforms have different requirements and best practices:

1. **Resolution and Aspect Ratio**: Most social media platforms and YouTube favor a 16:9 aspect ratio (widescreen), with resolutions like

1080p (1920x1080) being standard. However, for platforms like Instagram or TikTok, you might want to use a square (1:1) or vertical (9:16) aspect ratio. Make sure to choose the right resolution and aspect ratio for your target platform to avoid black bars or cropped content.

2. **File Size and Compression**: Large video files can be slow to upload and may not play smoothly on all devices. Most video editing tools allow you to compress your video during export, reducing file size without sacrificing too much quality. Aim for a balance between quality and file size, especially if you're uploading to platforms with file size limits.

3. **Frame Rate**: The standard frame rate for most videos is 24 to 30 frames per second (fps). However, if your animation has a lot of fast motion, you might want to go up to 60 fps for smoother playback. Keep in mind that higher frame rates can increase file size.

4. **Audio Quality**: Ensure your audio is clear and well-balanced. Most platforms support audio at 44.1 kHz or 48 kHz. Avoid using overly compressed audio files, as they can sound tinny or distorted.

5. **Platform-Specific Settings**: Different platforms might have specific settings that are optimal for uploading. For example, YouTube supports higher bitrates and longer videos, while Instagram might require shorter, smaller files. Check the guidelines for each platform before uploading to ensure the best quality.

Finalizing Your Video for Upload

With your video edited and optimized, the final step is preparing it for upload. Here's how to make sure your video is ready to go:

1. **Review the Final Edit**: Before exporting, review your video from start to finish. Check for any mistakes, awkward cuts, or timing issues. Make sure the transitions are smooth, the audio is clear, and the overall flow feels right.

2. **Exporting the Video**: When you're happy with the final edit, it's time to export the video. Choose the appropriate format (usually MP4 for most platforms) and the best quality settings for your needs. Make sure to save the file in a location that's easy to access when you're ready to upload.

3. **Create a Thumbnail**: A good thumbnail can make a big difference in attracting viewers. Choose a frame from your video or create a custom image that captures the essence of your animation. Use bold, clear text and bright colors to make it stand out. Many editing tools allow you to create thumbnails or you can use a design tool like Canva.

4. **Write a Description and Tags**: Whether you're uploading to YouTube, Instagram, or another platform, take the time to write a good description that tells viewers what your video is about. Use relevant tags and keywords to help your video get discovered in search results.

5. **Upload and Share**: Finally, upload your video to the platform of your choice. Once it's live, don't forget to share it across your social media channels to reach a wider audience. Engage with viewers by responding to comments and encouraging them to like, share, and subscribe.

By following these steps, you'll be able to edit and polish your animated videos, ensuring they look professional and are ready to capture the attention of your audience.

CHAPTER 6: SETTING UP YOUR YOUTUBE CHANNEL

Your YouTube channel is your digital storefront. It's where viewers will discover your content, decide whether to subscribe and engage with your videos. Setting up a professional and appealing channel is crucial to building your audience and making a strong first impression. In this chapter, we'll cover how to create a cohesive brand for your channel, design eye-catching thumbnails and channel art, write effective titles and descriptions, and use tags and keywords to optimize your content for search engines.

Creating a Professional Channel Brand

Branding your YouTube channel is about creating a consistent and recognizable identity that reflects your content and resonates with your target audience. Here's how to build a professional brand for your channel:

1. **Define Your Channel's Purpose**: Start by clarifying what your channel is about. Are you creating educational content, entertainment, tutorials, or vlogs? Defining your channel's purpose will help you create content that's focused and appealing to your target audience. Make sure your channel's name, logo, and overall design align with this purpose.

2. **Choose a Memorable Channel Name**: Your channel name should be unique, easy to remember, and reflective of your content. If possible, keep it short and avoid using numbers or special characters, which can make it harder for viewers to find you. If your preferred name is taken, try adding a relevant word or phrase that aligns with your niche.

3. **Design a Channel Logo**: Your logo is a key part of your brand identity. It should be simple, distinctive, and consistent with the style of your content. You can create a logo using free design tools like Canva or hire a designer if you want something more polished. Make sure your logo looks good at various sizes, as it will be used in small spaces like your channel icon.

4. **Create a Channel Description**: Your channel description should tell visitors what your channel is about and why they should subscribe. Keep it concise but informative. Include a brief overview of the type of content you create, your posting schedule, and any unique value you offer. You can also include links to your social media accounts, website, or other relevant platforms.

5. **Consistent Visual Style**: Choose a consistent color palette, font, and style for all your channel's visuals, including thumbnails, banners, and video intros. This consistency helps create a cohesive brand that's instantly recognizable to viewers.

Designing Thumbnails and Channel Art

Thumbnails and channel art are the first things viewers see when they visit your channel, so it's important to make them visually appealing and informative. Here's how to design effective thumbnails and channel art:

1. **Creating Eye-Catching Thumbnails**:
   - *Bold and Clear Images*: Use high-quality images that are clear and easy to see, even at small sizes. Close-ups of faces or objects tend to work well. Make sure the main subject of your thumbnail stands out and isn't cluttered by too many details.
   - *Use Contrasting Colors*: Bright, contrasting colors help your thumbnails stand out in the YouTube feed. Choose colors that complement each other and avoid using too many different shades that could make the thumbnail look chaotic.
   - *Add Text Wisely*: Include a few words of text on your thumbnail to give viewers a quick idea of what the video is about. Use large, bold fonts that are easy to read, and keep the text short—typically 2-4 words. Make sure the text doesn't cover important parts of the image.
   - *Consistency is Key*: To strengthen your brand identity, use a consistent style for your thumbnails. This could be through the use of similar colors, fonts, or layout. When viewers see a thumbnail in their feed, they should be able to recognize it as one of your videos.

2. **Designing Channel Art**:
   - *Channel Banner*: Your channel banner is the large image that appears at the top of your YouTube page. It should reflect your channel's personality and include your logo, tagline, or a brief description of what viewers can expect

from your content. Keep in mind that the banner will look different on desktop, mobile, and TV screens, so make sure important elements are centered and within the "safe zone."

- *Include a Call-to-Action*: If you have a posting schedule, consider including it in your banner (e.g., "New Videos Every Wednesday"). You can also encourage viewers to subscribe or follow you on social media.
- *Update Seasonally*: Refresh your channel art occasionally to keep it current, especially for seasonal content or special series. This shows that your channel is active and evolving.

Writing Effective Titles and Descriptions

Your video titles and descriptions are crucial for attracting viewers and helping YouTube understand what your video is about. Here's how to write titles and descriptions that perform well:

1. **Crafting Compelling Titles**:
   - *Be Clear and Specific*: Your title should clearly convey what the video is about. Use specific language that tells viewers exactly what they can expect, whether it's a tutorial, a review, or a story. For example, instead of a vague title like "Cool Animation," opt for something more descriptive like "How to Create a Simple 2D Animation in 5 Minutes."
   - *Include Keywords*: Use relevant keywords in your title to help your video appear in search results. Think about what your audience might be searching for and incorporate those terms naturally into your title.
   - *Keep It Short*: YouTube typically displays the first 60 characters of your title, so aim to keep it concise. If your title is too long, important information might be cut off, especially on mobile devices.
   - *Add Brackets or Parentheses*: Consider adding extra information in brackets or parentheses to increase click-through rates. For example, "Best Free Animation Software (2024 Edition)" or "Easy Animation Tutorial [Beginner-Friendly]."

2. **Writing Detailed Descriptions**:
   - *Start with a Strong Lead*: The first few lines of your description should grab attention and give a quick summary of what the video is about. These lines are the most important because they are visible in the search results and above the "Show More" button.

- *Include Keywords and Phrases*: Just like with titles, including relevant keywords in your description helps with SEO (Search Engine Optimization). Mention the main topics, tools, or techniques covered in the video.
- *Add Value*: Use the description to provide additional value to your viewers. Include links to related videos, timestamps for different sections of the video, or resources mentioned in the video.

- *Encourage Engagement*: At the end of your description, include a call-to-action encouraging viewers to like, comment, and subscribe. You can also ask questions to prompt discussion in the comments.

Using Tags and Keywords for SEO

SEO (Search Engine Optimization) is the process of making your videos easier to find in search results. By using the right tags and keywords, you can help YouTube understand what your video is about and increase the chances of it being discovered by new viewers.

1. **Choosing the Right Keywords**:
   - *Brainstorm Keywords*: Think about the main topics, themes, and terms related to your video. Use tools like Google Keyword Planner, YouTube's autocomplete feature, or platforms like TubeBuddy to find popular keywords that people are searching for.
   - *Include Long-Tail Keywords*: Long-tail keywords are more specific phrases that people might search for, like "best free animation software for beginners." These are often easier to rank for than broad terms and can help attract a more targeted audience.
   - *Use Keywords Naturally*: Incorporate your keywords naturally into your title, description, and tags. Don't overstuff your video with keywords, as this can look spammy and harm your ranking.

2. **Optimizing Tags**:
   - *Use Relevant Tags*: Tags are short keywords or phrases that describe your video. Include a mix of broad tags (e.g., "animation") and specific tags (e.g., "how to create 2D animations"). Make sure all the tags you use are relevant to your video's content.
   - *Use Variations of Keywords*: Include different variations of

your main keywords as tags. For example, if your video is about animation software, you might include tags like "animation tools," "best animation software," and "animation programs."

- *Check Competitors' Tags*: Tools like TubeBuddy or VidIQ can help you see what tags your competitors are using. This can give you ideas for additional tags that might help your video reach a wider audience.

3. **Monitor and Adjust**:
    - *Analyze Your Video's Performance*: Use YouTube Analytics to see how your videos are performing. Pay attention to which videos are getting the most views, likes, and comments, and see if there's a pattern in the keywords or tags you used.
    - *Refine Your Strategy*: If certain keywords or tags are consistently driving traffic, make them a regular part of your SEO strategy. If others aren't working as well, experiment with new keywords or try different approaches.

By effectively using tags, keywords, and SEO strategies, you can increase the visibility of your videos, making it easier for potential subscribers to find your content.

CHAPTER 7: UPLOADING AND OPTIMIZING YOUR VIDEOS

Once your video is edited and ready to go, the next crucial step is uploading and optimizing it for the best possible performance on YouTube. This chapter will guide you through the best practices for uploading your videos, using YouTube Studio to optimize them, adding subtitles and closed captions, setting up playlists and end screens, and understanding YouTube Analytics to track your success.

Best Practices for Uploading

Uploading your video to YouTube is straightforward, but there are some best practices you should follow to ensure your video is set up for success:

1. **Choose the Right File Format**: YouTube supports a variety of video formats, but the recommended format is MP4 with an H.264 codec and AAC audio. This combination offers high quality while keeping the file size manageable.

2. **Title Your Video Effectively**: As soon as you upload your video, you'll need to give it a title. Make sure your title is clear, concise, and includes relevant keywords to help your video show up in search results. Avoid clickbait titles—your title should accurately reflect the content of your video.

3. **Write a Detailed Description**: Your video description is an opportunity to provide more context about your content. Start with a strong introduction that includes your main keywords, and then go into more detail about what the video covers. Include links to related content, your social media, and any resources mentioned in the video.

4. **Use a Custom Thumbnail**: Always upload a custom thumbnail rather than relying on the automatically generated ones. A custom thumbnail that's visually appealing and relevant to your content can significantly increase your click-through rate.

5. **Set the Visibility**: You can choose to make your video public,

unlisted, or private. Public videos are available to everyone, unlisted videos can only be viewed by those with the link, and private videos are only accessible to you and people you choose. For most content, you'll want to set the video to public.

6. **Schedule Your Upload**: If you want your video to go live at a specific time, you can schedule it in advance. This is particularly useful if you've built a following and want to release videos at the same time each week.

Using YouTube Studio for Optimization

YouTube Studio is a powerful tool that allows you to manage your channel, track video performance, and optimize your content. Here's how to make the most of it:

1. **Edit Video Details**: After uploading, use YouTube Studio to fine-tune your video details. You can adjust the title, description, and tags, as well as add or change the thumbnail.

2. **Add Tags**: Tags help YouTube understand the content of your video and can improve your visibility in search results. Use a mix of broad and specific tags related to your content. For example, if your video is about animation software, your tags might include "animation," "animation software," "how to animate," and "best animation tools."

3. **Use Cards and End Screens**: Cards and end screens are interactive elements you can add to your video to keep viewers engaged and direct them to other content on your channel.
   - *Cards*: Cards can be added at any point in your video and can link to other videos, playlists, or even external websites (if you're part of the YouTube Partner Program).
   - *End Screens*: End screens appear in the last 5-20 seconds of your video. Use them to promote other videos, encourage subscriptions, or link to playlists. End screens are a great way to keep viewers on your channel and increase watch time.

4. **Enable Monetization**: If you're eligible for the YouTube Partner Program, you can enable monetization on your videos through YouTube Studio. This allows ads to run on your videos, generating revenue for your channel.

Adding Subtitles and Closed Captions

Subtitles and closed captions not only make your content more accessible to a wider audience, including those with hearing impairments, but they can also improve your video's SEO. Here's how to add them:

1. **Automatic Captions**: YouTube automatically generates captions for your videos using speech recognition. While this feature is convenient, it's not always 100% accurate. You can edit these captions in YouTube Studio to correct any mistakes.

2. **Upload Your Own Captions**: For more accuracy, consider creating your own subtitles or closed captions. You can upload a subtitle file (like .srt) directly to YouTube. There are free tools available online, such as Subtitle Edit or Amara, which can help you create these files.

3. **Translate Captions**: If you have an international audience, consider translating your captions into other languages. YouTube allows you to upload captions in multiple languages, making your content accessible to a global audience.

4. **Include Keywords in Captions**: While the primary purpose of captions is accessibility, they also contribute to your video's SEO. Make sure your captions accurately reflect the content of your video, including relevant keywords.

Setting Up Playlists and End Screens

Playlists and end screens are effective tools for increasing viewer retention and guiding your audience through more of your content. Here's how to use them:

1. **Creating Playlists**:
    -   *Group Similar Content*: Organize your videos into playlists based on themes or topics. For example, if you have a series of tutorials, group them into a "Beginner Animation Tutorials" playlist. This makes it easier for viewers to find related content and encourages binge-watching.
    -   *Optimize Playlist Titles and Descriptions*: Just like your video titles and descriptions, playlists should be optimized with relevant keywords. This helps them show up in YouTube search results.
    -   *Promote Playlists*: Include links to your playlists in video descriptions, cards, and end screens to drive traffic to them.

2. **Setting Up End Screens**:
    -   *Promote Relevant Videos*: Use end screens to promote videos that are closely related to the one just watched. This

increases the likelihood that viewers will keep watching your content.

- **Encourage Subscriptions**: Include a subscribe button in your end screen to make it easy for viewers to subscribe to your channel. You can also include a call-to-action in your video, asking viewers to subscribe.
- **Customize Your End Screens**: YouTube offers templates for end screens, but you can also customize them to match your brand. Consistent branding across your end screens reinforces your channel's identity.

Understanding YouTube Analytics

YouTube Analytics is an essential tool for understanding how your videos are performing and making data-driven decisions to improve your content. Here's how to use it effectively:

1. **Monitor Key Metrics**:
    - **Views and Watch Time**: These metrics give you a sense of how many people are watching your videos and how long they're staying engaged. Watch time is particularly important because it's a key factor in YouTube's algorithm.
    - **Audience Retention**: This shows you where viewers are dropping off in your video. If you notice a consistent drop-off at a certain point, you may want to re-evaluate the content or pacing of your videos.
    - **Click-Through Rate (CTR)**: This metric tells you how often people click on your video after seeing the thumbnail. A high CTR indicates that your thumbnails and titles are effective, while a low CTR may suggest that they need improvement.

2. **Understand Your Audience**:
    - **Demographics**: YouTube Analytics provides insights into the age, gender, and location of your viewers. Understanding who your audience is can help you tailor your content to better meet their interests.
    - **Traffic Sources**: This tells you where your views are coming from—whether it's YouTube search, suggested videos, or external websites. Knowing your traffic sources can help you optimize your videos for the platforms and channels that drive the most views.
    - **Engagement**: Look at likes, comments, shares, and subscriber growth to see how your audience is interacting

with your content. High engagement is a good sign that your content is resonating with viewers.

3. **Use Data to Improve**:
   - *A/B Testing*: Experiment with different thumbnails, titles, and descriptions to see what works best. You can compare the performance of different videos to identify what elements contribute to higher engagement and views.
   - *Set Goals*: Use your analytics to set specific goals for your channel. Whether it's increasing your watch time, improving your CTR, or gaining more subscribers, having clear goals will help you focus your efforts and track your progress.

CHAPTER 8: PROMOTING YOUR ANIMATED VIDEOS

Creating high-quality animated videos is just the beginning. To grow your YouTube channel and reach a wider audience, effective promotion is key. In this chapter, we'll explore strategies for promoting your videos, from cross-promotion on social media to engaging with your audience and building a community around your content.

Cross-Promotion on Social Media

Social media platforms are powerful tools for promoting your YouTube videos and driving traffic to your channel. Here's how to leverage them effectively:

1. **Choose the Right Platforms**: Not all social media platforms are created equal. Choose the platforms where your target audience is most active. For example, Instagram and TikTok are great for sharing short, eye-catching clips, while Facebook and Twitter are ideal for longer-form content and discussions .

2. **Tailor Your Content**: Each platform has its own style and audience, so tailor your content accordingly. On Instagram, you might post a short teaser of your video with a link to the full version on YouTube. On Twitter, share a compelling quote or fact from the video with a direct link.

3. **Use Hashtags Wisely**: Hashtags help your content get discovered by people who are interested in your niche. Research popular hashtags in your industry and include them in your posts. Tools like Hashtagify or the built-in search functions on social media platforms can help you find relevant hashtags.

4. **Create Teaser Clips**: Create short teaser clips or GIFs from your videos to share on social media. These snippets should be intriguing and leave viewers wanting more, encouraging them to click through to your full video on YouTube.

5. **Engage with Your Followers**: Don't just post and forget—engage with your followers by responding to comments, liking posts, and participating in discussions. The more you interact with your audience, the more likely they are to share your content and support your channel.

6. **Share Consistently**: Regularly share your videos across your social media platforms. Consistency is key to keeping your audience engaged and growing your reach. Use a social media scheduling tool like Buffer or Hootsuite to plan and automate your posts.

Collaborations and Networking

Collaborating with other creators and networking within your industry can significantly boost your visibility and subscriber count. Here's how to get started:

1. **Identify Potential Collaborators**: Look for creators in your niche or related fields who have a similar audience. Collaborations can range from shoutouts and guest appearances to co-created content. For example, you could create a joint animation project or participate in a Q&A session on each other's channels.

2. **Reach Out Professionally**: When reaching out to potential collaborators, be professional and respectful. Explain why you think a collaboration would be mutually beneficial, and propose specific ideas for how you can work together. Make sure to highlight the value you can offer to their audience.

3. **Leverage Existing Networks**: If you're active in online communities or social media groups related to your niche, use these networks to find collaboration opportunities. Engage with other members, share your work, and participate in discussions to build relationships.

4. **Attend Industry Events**: Virtual or in-person industry events, such as conferences, webinars, or meetups, are great places to network with other creators and professionals. These events offer opportunities to learn, share your expertise, and connect with potential collaborators.

5. **Cross-Promote Content**: When collaborating, make sure both parties promote the content across their channels and social media platforms. This cross-promotion exposes your video to a new audience and can lead to increased subscribers and views.

Utilizing YouTube Ads and Promotions

YouTube offers several paid promotion options to help your videos reach a larger audience. While organic growth is important, a strategic ad campaign can accelerate your channel's success:

1. **YouTube Ads Overview**: YouTube offers different types of ads, including TrueView ads (skippable ads that play before, during, or after videos), Discovery ads (which appear in search results and on the YouTube homepage), and Bumper ads (short, non-skippable ads). Each type of ad serves a different purpose, so choose the one that aligns with your goals.

2. **Setting Up a Campaign**: To start promoting your videos with YouTube Ads, you'll need to set up a campaign through Google Ads. Define your target audience based on demographics, interests, and behaviors. You can also target specific keywords or placements (such as appearing on videos related to your niche).

3. **Budgeting for Ads**: Decide on a budget for your ad campaign. You can set a daily budget and choose between cost-per-view (CPV) or cost-per-click (CPC) bidding strategies. Start with a small budget to test your ads, and scale up as you see what works.

4. **Monitoring Ad Performance**: Use Google Ads and YouTube Analytics to track the performance of your ads. Pay attention to metrics like views, click-through rates, and conversion rates. This data will help you refine your targeting and improve future campaigns.

5. **Promote Specific Content**: Use YouTube Ads to promote your best-performing videos, channel trailers, or any special content you want to highlight. Ads are also effective for promoting new videos to ensure they gain traction quickly.

Engaging with Your Audience

Building a loyal audience requires more than just great content—you need to actively engage with your viewers and create a sense of community:

1. **Respond to Comments**: Make it a habit to respond to comments on your videos. Acknowledge positive feedback, answer questions, and thank viewers for their support. Engaging in conversations with your audience shows that you value their input and encourages them to

stay involved.

2. **Ask for Feedback**: Invite your viewers to share their thoughts on your videos and suggest topics for future content. This not only provides you with valuable insights but also makes your audience feel like they're part of your creative process.

3. **Host Live Streams**: Live streaming is a powerful way to connect with your audience in real-time. Use live streams to answer questions, share behind-the-scenes content, or discuss topics related to your videos. Live interactions build a stronger connection with your audience and can increase viewer loyalty.

4. **Create Polls and Surveys**: Use YouTube's community tab, Instagram Stories, or other platforms to create polls and surveys. Ask your audience what type of content they want to see or gather their opinions on different topics. This engagement can lead to higher viewer satisfaction and more views.

5. **Encourage User-Generated Content**: Invite your viewers to create their own content related to your videos. This could be fan art, response videos, or social media posts. Feature their work in your videos or share it on your social media channels to show appreciation and foster a sense of community.

Building a Community Around Your Content

Building a community is about creating a space where your viewers feel connected to you and to each other. A strong community can lead to higher engagement, more loyal subscribers, and greater success for your channel:

1. **Create a Consistent Posting Schedule**: Regular uploads help build anticipation and keep your audience engaged. Whether you post weekly, bi-weekly, or monthly, consistency is key to maintaining viewer interest and growing your community.

2. **Develop a Unique Voice**: Your personality and voice are what make your channel unique. Be authentic in your interactions and content, and let your passion for your subject matter shine through. A strong, relatable voice helps viewers feel more connected to you.

3. **Foster Interaction Among Viewers**: Encourage your audience to interact with each other in the comments section. Ask open-ended questions in your videos that spark discussions, or create content that

invites viewers to share their experiences and opinions.

4. **Use the Community Tab**: If your channel has access to YouTube's community tab, use it to engage with your audience between video uploads. Share updates, behind-the-scenes content, polls, and more. The community tab is a great way to keep the conversation going and build a sense of belonging.

5. **Host Contests and Giveaways**: Contests and giveaways are effective ways to boost engagement and reward your loyal viewers. You could ask viewers to create content related to your videos, share your channel, or answer trivia questions. Make sure the prizes are relevant to your audience's interests.

6. **Create a Patreon or Membership Program**: If you have a dedicated following, consider creating a Patreon or YouTube membership program. These platforms allow your biggest fans to support you financially in exchange for exclusive content, perks, or behind-the-scenes access. A membership program can strengthen your community and provide you with a steady income stream.

By implementing these strategies, you'll be able to promote your animated videos effectively, engage with your audience, and build a thriving community around your content. This not only increases your channel's growth but also fosters a loyal viewer base that will support you for the long term.

CHAPTER 9: MONETIZATION STRATEGIES

Creating engaging animated videos and building a loyal audience is incredibly rewarding, but the next step is to turn your passion into a source of income. YouTube offers several ways to monetize your content, allowing you to generate revenue and potentially even make a living from your channel. In this chapter, we'll explore various monetization strategies, including ad revenue, affiliate marketing, sponsored content, selling merchandise, crowdfunding, and more.

Ad Revenue and YouTube Partner Program

One of the most common ways to earn money on YouTube is through ad revenue, which is made possible by joining the YouTube Partner Program (YPP). Here's how it works:

1. **Joining the YouTube Partner Program (YPP):**
   - *Eligibility Requirements*: To qualify for the YouTube Partner Program, your channel must have at least 1,000 subscribers and 4,000 watch hours over the past 12 months. You also need to comply with all of YouTube's policies and guidelines, and have an AdSense account linked to your channel.
   - *Applying for YPP*: Once you meet the eligibility criteria, you can apply for YPP through YouTube Studio. YouTube will review your channel to ensure it meets the guidelines. This process can take a few weeks.

2. **Understanding Ad Revenue:**
   - *How Ads Work*: Once you're accepted into YPP, YouTube will start showing ads on your videos. You earn money whenever viewers interact with these ads (e.g., by watching the ad for a certain length of time or clicking on it). The amount you earn depends on factors like the number of views, the type of ad, and the viewer's location.
   - *Types of Ads*: YouTube offers several types of ads, including display ads (which appear next to your video), overlay ads (which appear as banners on the video),

skippable video ads (which viewers can skip after 5 seconds), and non-skippable video ads (which viewers must watch in full).

- **Revenue Sharing**: YouTube takes a 45% cut of the ad revenue, and you keep the remaining 55%. While this might seem like a lot, ad revenue can still be a significant source of income, especially as your channel grows.

3. **Maximizing Ad Revenue**:
   - **Create Longer Videos**: Videos that are at least 8 minutes long allow you to place mid-roll ads, which can increase your ad revenue. However, don't sacrifice quality for length—only make your videos longer if it adds value to your content.
   - **Increase Watch Time**: The more time viewers spend watching your videos, the more ads they'll see, which can boost your revenue. Focus on creating engaging content that keeps viewers watching until the end.
   - **Target High-CPM Niches**: Some niches, such as finance, technology, and business, tend to have higher CPMs (cost per thousand impressions) because advertisers are willing to pay more to reach these audiences. If it aligns with your interests, consider creating content in these niches.

Affiliate Marketing and Sponsored Content

Affiliate marketing and sponsored content are two powerful monetization strategies that allow you to earn money by promoting products or services in your videos.

1. **Affiliate Marketing**:
   - **How It Works**: With affiliate marketing, you promote a product or service in your video and include a unique affiliate link in your description. When someone clicks on the link and makes a purchase, you earn a commission.
   - **Choosing Affiliate Programs**: Look for affiliate programs that align with your content and audience. Amazon Associates is a popular option because it offers a wide range of products, but there are many other programs available in various niches. Platforms like ShareASale, CJ Affiliate, and Rakuten are great places to find affiliate programs.
   - **Integrating Affiliate Links**: Mention the product or service naturally in your video, and explain why you recommend it. Always disclose that the link is an affiliate link to maintain

transparency with your audience.

2. **Sponsored Content**:
   - *What It Is*: Sponsored content involves partnering with a brand or company to create a video that promotes their product or service. In exchange, the brand pays you a fee or provides you with free products.
   - *Finding Sponsorships*: As your channel grows, brands may reach out to you for sponsorships. You can also actively seek out sponsorships by contacting companies that align with your content. Platforms like Famebit and Grapevine can help connect you with potential sponsors.
   - *Negotiating Sponsorships*: When negotiating a sponsorship deal, consider factors like the length of the video, the level of promotion, and the size of your audience. Make sure the compensation reflects the value you bring to the brand. Always be clear about the terms of the agreement, including deliverables, deadlines, and payment.
   - *Maintaining Authenticity*: Only accept sponsorships that align with your values and that you genuinely believe in. Your audience's trust is crucial, so it's important to promote products and services that you can confidently recommend.

Creating and Selling Merch

Selling merchandise (merch) is another great way to monetize your channel and build a deeper connection with your audience. Here's how to get started:

1. **Designing Your Merch**:
   - *Create Branded Products*: Start by designing products that reflect your brand and appeal to your audience. This could include T-shirts, hoodies, mugs, stickers, and more. Use your channel's logo, catchphrases, or unique designs that resonate with your viewers.
   - *Keep It Simple*: You don't need a wide range of products to start—focus on a few high-quality items that your audience will love. As your merch line gains popularity, you can expand your offerings.

2. **Choosing a Merch Platform**:
   - *Print-on-Demand Services*: Print-on-demand services like Teespring, Redbubble, and Merch by Amazon allow you to design and sell products without needing to hold inventory.

When someone orders a product, the service handles the printing, shipping, and customer service.

- *E-commerce Platforms*: If you want more control over your merch, consider setting up an online store using platforms like Shopify or WooCommerce. This allows you to manage your inventory and offer a wider range of products.

3. **Promoting Your Merch:**
   - *Integrate Merch in Your Videos*: Wear or use your merch in your videos, and mention where viewers can purchase it. You can also create dedicated merch videos to showcase new products or offer limited-time discounts.
   - *Use YouTube Merch Shelf*: If you're part of the YouTube Partner Program and meet the eligibility criteria, you can use the Merch Shelf feature to display your products directly under your videos, making it easy for viewers to buy.

4. *Offering Exclusive Items*: To encourage purchases, consider offering exclusive items or limited-edition products. This creates a sense of urgency and makes your merch feel special to your audience.

Crowdfunding and Patreon

Crowdfunding and membership platforms like Patreon offer another way to monetize your channel by allowing your most dedicated fans to support you directly:

1. **Crowdfunding Campaigns:**
   - *How It Works*: Crowdfunding involves raising money from your audience for a specific project, like creating a new series or upgrading your equipment. Platforms like Kickstarter, Indiegogo, and GoFundMe are popular for running crowdfunding campaigns.
   - *Creating a Campaign*: When setting up a crowdfunding campaign, clearly outline your goals, what you plan to create, and how the funds will be used. Offer rewards or perks for different donation levels, such as exclusive content, shoutouts, or early access to videos.
   - *Promoting Your Campaign*: Use your YouTube channel and social media platforms to promote your campaign. Regularly update your audience on the campaign's progress and thank contributors for their support.

2. **Patreon Memberships**:
  - *How Patreon Works*: Patreon allows creators to offer exclusive content and perks to their subscribers (patrons) in exchange for a monthly subscription fee. Patrons can choose from different membership tiers, each offering different rewards.
  - *Setting Up Your Patreon Page*: Create a Patreon page that explains what you offer and why viewers should support you. Define your membership tiers and rewards, such as early access to videos, behind-the-scenes content, personalized shoutouts, or exclusive live streams.
  - **Promoting Your Patreon**: Mention your Patreon page in your videos and include links in your video descriptions and channel banner. Regularly engage with your patrons and deliver on the promised rewards to maintain their support.

3. **Maintaining Transparency**: Be transparent with your patrons about how the funds are being used and what they can expect in return. Building trust with your supporters is essential for maintaining a successful crowdfunding or membership campaign.

Building Multiple Streams of Income

Relying on just one income source can be risky, especially if changes to YouTube's algorithms or policies affect your ad revenue. Building multiple streams of income can provide financial stability and help you grow your earnings over time:

1. **Diversify Your Income**:
  - *Combine Strategies*: Use a combination of ad revenue, affiliate marketing, sponsored content, merch sales, and crowdfunding to generate income from different sources. This diversification can help protect you against fluctuations in any one revenue stream.
  - *Explore New Platforms*: In addition to YouTube, consider expanding your presence on other platforms like Instagram, TikTok, or a personal blog. These platforms offer additional monetization opportunities and help you reach a broader audience.

2. **Create Digital Products**:
  - *Sell Online Courses*: If you're an expert in your niche, consider creating and selling online courses. Platforms like

Udemy, Skillshare, or Teachable allow you to reach a wide audience and earn money from your knowledge.

- *Offer Ebooks or Guides*: Create and sell digital products like ebooks, guides, or templates related to your content. These products can provide value to your audience while generating additional income.

3. **License Your Content**:
   - *Sell Stock Footage*: If you create high-quality animations, consider selling your footage on stock websites like Shutterstock, Pond5, or Adobe Stock. This allows you to earn passive income from your work.
   - *License Your Animations*: You can also license your animations to other creators, businesses, or educational institutions. This can be a lucrative way to monetize your content, especially if you have a unique style or niche.

4. **Invest in Passive Income Streams**:
   - *Build a Blog or Website*: Create a blog or website that complements your YouTube channel. Monetize it with ads, affiliate links, or digital products. A blog can also help drive traffic to your videos and improve your online presence.
   - *Explore Passive Income Opportunities*: Consider other passive income opportunities like creating print-on-demand products, developing an app, or investing in dividend-paying stocks. These strategies can supplement your YouTube income and provide long-term financial security.

By building multiple streams of income, you can create a sustainable and profitable business around your YouTube channel. This not only increases your earning potential but also provides financial stability, allowing you to focus on creating the content you love.

CHAPTER 10: EXPANDING BEYOND YOUTUBE

While YouTube is a powerful platform for sharing your animated content and building an audience, there are many other opportunities to expand your reach and monetize your skills. This chapter will guide you through strategies for repurposing your content for other platforms, creating animated content for brands and clients, leveraging your animation skills for freelance work, and developing long-term growth strategies for your animation business.

Repurposing Content for Other Platforms

Expanding your presence beyond YouTube allows you to reach new audiences and diversify your content strategy. Here's how to repurpose your YouTube videos for other popular platforms:

1. **Instagram:**
    - *IGTV and Reels*: Instagram's IGTV is perfect for sharing longer videos, while Reels is ideal for shorter, more engaging clips. You can repurpose sections of your YouTube videos or create teaser clips to draw people to your channel. Use Instagram's built-in tools to add captions, stickers, and effects that suit the platform's style.
    - *Stories and Posts*: Share shorter clips, behind-the-scenes content, or still frames from your videos as Instagram Stories or posts. Add engaging captions, questions, or polls to encourage interaction from your followers.

2. **TikTok:**
    - *Short-Form Content*: TikTok is all about short, snappy content. Break down your longer YouTube videos into bite-sized segments that highlight the most interesting or entertaining parts. Use TikTok's editing tools to add music, text overlays, and effects that resonate with the platform's audience.
    - *Trends and Challenges*: Participate in TikTok trends and challenges by adapting your animations to fit popular themes

or hashtags. This can help your content go viral and reach a broader audience.

3. **Facebook**:
   - *Facebook Video and Stories*: Upload your full YouTube videos to Facebook to tap into its vast user base. You can also create shorter clips or highlights to share in Facebook Stories. Engage with your audience by responding to comments and participating in discussions on your posts.
   - *Facebook Groups*: Join or create Facebook groups related to your niche. Share your content within these groups to connect with like-minded individuals and attract new viewers to your channel.

4. **Twitter**:
   - *Tweet Clips and Teasers*: Share short clips, GIFs, or key takeaways from your YouTube videos on Twitter. Use relevant hashtags and tag influencers or communities that might be interested in your content.
   - *Engage in Conversations*: Twitter is a great platform for engaging in real-time conversations. Use it to share updates, ask questions, or participate in trending discussions related to your niche.

5. **Pinterest**:
   - *Create Pins*: Pinterest is an underrated platform for video content. Create pins that link back to your YouTube videos, blog posts, or online store. Use eye-catching thumbnails and compelling descriptions to attract clicks.
   - *Organize Boards*: Create boards that categorize your content by theme or topic. This makes it easier for users to discover and save your pins, driving traffic back to your YouTube channel or website.

By repurposing your content across multiple platforms, you can reach new audiences, increase your visibility, and drive more traffic to your YouTube channel.

Creating Animated Content for Brands and Clients

As you gain experience and build your portfolio, creating animated content for brands and clients can become a lucrative part of your business. Here's how to get started:

1. **Build a Portfolio:**
   - *Showcase Your Best Work*: Create a portfolio that highlights your best animations, including a variety of styles and formats. This could be a dedicated website, a Vimeo channel, or even a well-organized YouTube playlist. Make sure your portfolio is easy to navigate and demonstrates your skills clearly.
   - *Include Case Studies*: If you've worked with brands or clients before, include case studies that showcase the results of your work. This could include metrics like engagement rates, conversions, or viewer feedback. Case studies help potential clients see the value you can bring to their projects.

2. **Pitching to Brands:**
   - *Identify Potential Clients*: Start by identifying brands or companies that align with your style and expertise. Look for businesses that are active in content marketing, have a strong online presence, or are in industries that rely heavily on visual content.
   - *Craft a Compelling Pitch*: When reaching out to potential clients, personalize your pitch to their needs. Highlight how your animations can help them achieve their goals, whether it's increasing brand awareness, engaging their audience, or explaining complex concepts. Include examples from your portfolio that are relevant to their industry.
   - *Offer a Range of Services*: Be clear about the services you offer, such as explainer videos, social media animations, or promotional content. Offering a range of options gives clients flexibility and makes you a more attractive partner.

3. **Delivering High-Quality Work:**
   - *Understand the Client's Vision*: Before starting a project, take the time to fully understand the client's vision, goals, and target audience. This ensures that the final product aligns with their expectations.
   - *Communicate Regularly*: Keep the client informed throughout the production process. Provide updates, share drafts, and be open to feedback. Clear communication helps build trust and ensures the project runs smoothly.
   - *Exceed Expectations*: Whenever possible, go above and beyond to deliver high-quality work. This could mean adding extra polish to the animation, delivering ahead of schedule,

or including a bonus element that enhances the final product. Satisfied clients are more likely to hire you again and refer you to others.

Leveraging Your Animation Skills for Freelance Work

Freelancing is a flexible way to monetize your animation skills and work on a variety of interesting projects. Here's how to succeed as a freelance animator:

1. **Join Freelance Platforms**:
   - ***Upwork and Fiverr***: These platforms are popular for freelancers and offer a wide range of animation gigs. Create a profile that highlights your skills, experience, and portfolio. Be sure to include relevant keywords so clients can find you easily.
   - ***Behance and Dribbble***: While these platforms are more focused on design, they're great for showcasing your animation work and connecting with potential clients. Use these platforms to build your network and discover job opportunities.
   - ***Freelancer.com***: Similar to Upwork, Freelancer.com connects freelancers with clients looking for animation work. Bid on projects that match your skills and set competitive rates to attract clients.

2. **Set Competitive Rates**:
   - ***Research the Market***: Before setting your rates, research what other animators are charging for similar work. Your rates should reflect your experience, the complexity of the project, and the value you provide to the client.
   - ***Consider Project-Based Pricing***: Instead of charging by the hour, consider offering project-based pricing. This gives clients a clear understanding of the total cost upfront and allows you to price your services based on the value of the final product.
   - ***Offer Tiered Pricing***: Provide different pricing tiers based on the scope of the project. For example, you could offer a basic package with minimal features, a standard package with additional elements, and a premium package with full customization. Tiered pricing gives clients options and can help you upsell more comprehensive services.

3. **Manage Your Time and Workflow**:
   - ***Use Project Management Tools***: Tools like Trello, Asana,

or Monday.com can help you manage multiple projects, track deadlines, and communicate with clients. Staying organized is crucial for delivering work on time and maintaining a professional reputation.

- *Set Boundaries*: Freelancing offers flexibility, but it's important to set boundaries to avoid burnout. Establish clear working hours, set realistic deadlines, and communicate your availability to clients.
- *Continuously Improve Your Skills*: The animation industry is constantly evolving, so it's important to keep your skills up to date. Invest time in learning new techniques, exploring different software, and staying informed about industry trends. The more versatile you are, the more attractive you'll be to potential clients.

Long-Term Growth Strategies for Your Animation Business

Building a sustainable and successful animation business requires long-term planning and strategic thinking. Here are some strategies to help you grow and scale your business:

1. **Expand Your Services**:
   - *Offer Consultation Services*: As you gain experience, consider offering consultation services to businesses or individuals who need advice on animation projects, content strategy, or visual storytelling. This can open up new revenue streams and position you as an expert in your field.
   - *Develop Online Courses*: Share your knowledge by creating online courses or workshops that teach others how to animate or improve their animation skills. Platforms like Udemy, Skillshare, or Teachable make it easy to reach a global audience and generate passive income.
   - *Create Digital Products*: Develop and sell digital products like animation templates, motion graphics packs, or educational resources. These products can be sold on your website, on marketplaces like Gumroad, or through stock footage sites, providing you with a steady income stream.

2. **Build a Team**:
   - *Outsource or Hire*: As your business grows, you may find it challenging to handle all aspects of production on your own. Consider outsourcing certain tasks (like video editing, sound design, or social media management) or hiring freelancers to

help with larger projects. Building a team allows you to take on more clients and focus on high-level tasks.

- *Invest in Training*: If you decide to hire employees or freelancers, invest in their training to ensure they meet your standards. This will help maintain the quality of your work and ensure consistency across all projects.

3. **Focus on Branding and Marketing**:
     - *Develop a Strong Brand Identity*: Your brand is more than just a logo—it's how clients perceive your business. Invest in professional branding, including a logo, website, and marketing materials that reflect your style and values.
     - *Leverage Content Marketing*: Use content marketing to establish yourself as a thought leader in the animation industry. Start a blog, create video tutorials, or write guest posts for industry websites. Providing valuable content helps attract clients and build trust.
     - *Network and Build Relationships*: Networking is key to growing your business. Attend industry events, join online communities, and collaborate with other creators. Building strong relationships can lead to new opportunities, referrals, and partnerships.

4. **Plan for Financial Stability**:
     - *Diversify Your Income Streams*: As mentioned earlier, relying on a single source of income can be risky. Diversify your income by combining ad revenue, client work, digital products, and other monetization strategies.
     - *Save and Invest*: Set aside a portion of your earnings for savings and investments. This financial cushion can help you navigate slow periods, invest in new equipment, or expand your business when opportunities arise.
     - *Set Long-Term Goals*: Establish clear long-term goals for your business, whether it's increasing your revenue, expanding your client base, or launching a new product line. Regularly review and adjust your goals as your business evolves.

By implementing these long-term growth strategies, you can build a sustainable animation business that not only supports your creative ambitions but also provides financial security and opportunities for expansion.

CHAPTER 11: TROUBLESHOOTING AND OVERCOMING CHALLENGES

No matter how experienced you are in animation or content creation, challenges are inevitable. Whether it's dealing with technical issues, managing your time, staying motivated, or adapting to changes on platforms like YouTube, overcoming these challenges is key to long-term success. In this chapter, we'll explore common animation mistakes and how to avoid them, strategies for managing time and resources, tips for staying motivated and consistent, and how to adapt to algorithm changes and platform updates.

Common Animation Mistakes and How to Avoid Them

Even seasoned animators can make mistakes that affect the quality of their work. Here's how to identify and avoid some of the most common pitfalls:

1. **Overcomplicating Your Animations:**
   - *The Mistake*: It's easy to get carried away with complex movements, intricate details, or excessive effects, but this can overwhelm your audience and lead to a cluttered final product.
   - *How to Avoid It*: Focus on simplicity and clarity. Each element in your animation should have a purpose. Ask yourself if a movement or detail adds value to the story or message—if not, consider simplifying it. Clean, straightforward animations often have a greater impact.

2. **Ignoring the Importance of Timing:**
   - *The Mistake*: Poor timing can make your animations feel sluggish, rushed, or unnatural. This is often a result of not paying enough attention to the pacing of movements or transitions.
   - *How to Avoid It*: Study the principles of timing in animation. Practice adjusting the speed of different actions to see how they change the feel of your animation. Use easing in and easing out (gradual acceleration or deceleration) to create more natural movements. Reviewing your work in real-time or slow motion can also help you fine-tune the timing.

3. **Neglecting Sound Design**:
    - *The Mistake*: Overlooking sound design can result in animations that feel flat or incomplete. Without appropriate sound effects or music, your animation may not fully engage your audience.
    - *How to Avoid It*: Treat sound as an integral part of your animation. Invest time in finding or creating sound effects that match the actions in your animation. Choose music that complements the mood and enhances the overall experience. Sync audio carefully with visual elements to ensure a cohesive final product.

4. **Inconsistent Character Design**:
    - *The Mistake*: Inconsistencies in character design, such as changing proportions, colors, or features, can distract viewers and break the immersion of your animation.
    - *How to Avoid It*: Create character sheets that include multiple views (front, side, back) and key expressions for each character. Refer to these sheets throughout the animation process to maintain consistency. Regularly check your work against these references to ensure your characters remain consistent from start to finish.

5. **Overloading on Effects and Filters**:
    - *The Mistake*: Using too many effects or filters can make your animation look over-processed and detract from the core content.
    - *How to Avoid It*: Use effects sparingly and purposefully. Each effect should enhance the storytelling or visual appeal, not overwhelm it. Consider the overall aesthetic of your animation and choose effects that complement your style without overpowering the main elements.

Managing Time and Resources Effectively

Balancing the demands of animation production with limited time and resources can be challenging. Here are some strategies to help you stay on track:

1. **Plan Your Projects**:
    - *Create a Production Schedule*: Break down your animation project into smaller tasks and set deadlines for each one. This could include scripting, storyboarding, character design,

animation, sound design, and editing. A clear schedule helps you manage your time effectively and ensures you stay on track.

- *Use Project Management Tools*: Tools like Trello, Asana, or Monday.com can help you organize tasks, set priorities, and track your progress. These tools are especially useful if you're working on multiple projects or collaborating with others.

2. **Prioritize Tasks**:
   - *Focus on High-Impact Tasks*: Identify the tasks that will have the biggest impact on the quality of your animation or the success of your channel. Prioritize these tasks to ensure they receive the attention they need.
   - *Avoid Multitasking*: Multitasking can lead to decreased productivity and lower-quality work. Instead, focus on one task at a time, completing it before moving on to the next. This approach helps you maintain a higher level of focus and produce better results.

3. **Optimize Your Workflow**:
   - *Use Templates and Pre-Sets*: Save time by creating templates or using pre-sets for recurring tasks, such as intros, outros, or commonly used effects. This allows you to work more efficiently and maintain consistency across your videos.
   - *Batch Similar Tasks*: Group similar tasks together and complete them in batches. For example, dedicate one day to scripting multiple videos, another to recording voiceovers, and another to editing. This reduces the time spent switching between tasks and helps you work more efficiently.

4. **Allocate Resources Wisely**:
   - *Set a Budget*: If you're working with limited resources, set a budget for each project. This might include costs for software, sound effects, music licenses, or outsourcing certain tasks. Keeping track of expenses helps you stay within your means and avoid overspending.
   - *Outsource When Necessary*: If you're struggling to manage all aspects of production, consider outsourcing certain tasks. Freelancers can help with specific tasks like sound design, editing, or creating assets, allowing you to focus on the core elements of your animation.

Staying Motivated and Consistent

Consistency and motivation are key to building a successful animation channel, but maintaining them over time can be difficult. Here's how to stay on track:

1. **Set Realistic Goals**:
   - *Break Down Big Goals*: Large goals can be overwhelming, so break them down into smaller, achievable steps. For example, if your goal is to release a new video every week, break it down into daily tasks like scripting on Monday, animating on Tuesday, and editing on Wednesday.
   - *Celebrate Small Wins*: Recognize and celebrate your progress, even the small victories. Whether it's completing a challenging scene or reaching a subscriber milestone, acknowledging your achievements helps keep you motivated.

2. **Develop a Routine**:
   - *Create a Consistent Schedule*: Establish a daily or weekly routine that includes dedicated time for animation. Consistency in your work schedule helps you build momentum and maintain progress over time.
   - *Avoid Burnout*: Take breaks when needed and don't push yourself too hard. Overworking can lead to burnout, which can derail your progress and make it difficult to stay motivated. Balance work with relaxation and hobbies to keep your creative energy high.

3. **Seek Inspiration**:
   - *Consume Creative Content*: Watch other animations, read books, or explore art that inspires you. Exposure to different styles and ideas can spark creativity and motivate you to try new things in your own work.
   - *Join Creative Communities*: Connect with other animators and creators through online forums, social media groups, or local meetups. Sharing your work and receiving feedback from peers can provide motivation and a sense of community.

4. **Stay Positive**:
   - *Focus on Growth*: Instead of comparing yourself to others, focus on your own growth and improvement. Celebrate the progress you've made and use any challenges as learning

opportunities.

- ***Practice Gratitude***: Reflect on what you enjoy about animation and the journey you've taken so far. Practicing gratitude can help you maintain a positive mindset and stay motivated, even during challenging times.

Adapting to Algorithm Changes and Platform Updates

YouTube and other social media platforms frequently update their algorithms and features, which can impact how your content is discovered and engaged with. Adapting to these changes is crucial for maintaining and growing your audience:

1. **Stay Informed**:
   - ***Follow Industry News***: Keep up with the latest news about YouTube and other platforms by following industry blogs, social media accounts, and YouTube's official updates. Staying informed helps you anticipate changes and adjust your strategy accordingly.
   - ***Participate in Creator Communities***: Join online communities where creators discuss algorithm changes, share tips, and offer support. These communities can provide valuable insights and help you navigate platform updates.

2. **Analyze Your Performance**:
   - ***Use YouTube Analytics***: Regularly review your YouTube Analytics to understand how algorithm changes are affecting your channel. Pay attention to metrics like watch time, click-through rate, and subscriber growth to identify trends and make data-driven decisions.
   - ***Experiment with Content***: If you notice a decline in views or engagement, experiment with different types of content, formats, or posting schedules. Test new ideas and see how your audience responds. Flexibility is key to adapting to changes in platform algorithms.

3. **Optimize Your Content**:
   - ***Focus on Quality and Relevance***: High-quality, relevant content is more likely to perform well, regardless of algorithm changes. Focus on creating videos that provide value to your audience, answer their questions, or entertain them.
   - ***Leverage SEO Best Practices***: Continue to optimize your

titles, descriptions, tags, and thumbnails to ensure your videos are discoverable. SEO best practices remain important even as algorithms evolve.

4. **Diversify Your Platforms**:
   - *Expand Beyond YouTube*: Relying solely on YouTube can be risky, especially if algorithm changes negatively impact your channel. Diversify your presence by sharing content on other platforms like Instagram, TikTok, or your own website.
   - *Build a Direct Audience*: Consider building an email list or creating a community on platforms like Patreon or Discord. This allows you to maintain direct communication with your audience, independent of platform algorithms.

By staying informed, analyzing your performance, and adapting your strategies, you can successfully navigate platform changes and continue to grow your audience.

CHAPTER 12: EXPLORING ADVANCED ANIMATION SOFTWARE AND AI VIDEO GENERATORS

As technology continues to evolve, the animation industry is being revolutionized by AI-powered video generators and advanced software. These tools are not only transforming how creators produce content but also opening up new possibilities for efficiency and creativity. In this chapter, we'll delve into the latest AI video generators, how they work, and how you can integrate them into your workflow to enhance your animation projects.

Understanding AI Video Generators

AI video generators use artificial intelligence and machine learning algorithms to create animations and videos based on user input. These tools significantly reduce the time and effort required to produce high-quality animations, making them accessible even to those with limited technical skills. Here's an overview of how they function:

1. **How AI Video Generators Work:**
   - *Input-Based Generation*: AI video generators typically begin with user input, such as text descriptions, images, or basic sketches. The AI processes this input and generates a video or animation based on learned patterns from vast datasets.
   - *Machine Learning Algorithms*: These tools leverage machine learning algorithms trained on extensive datasets of images, videos, and animations. The AI can recognize patterns and replicate them, producing realistic animations that match user specifications.
   - *Customization and Control*: While AI video generators automate much of the animation process, they often offer customization options. Users can adjust parameters like style, pacing, and color schemes to ensure the final product aligns with their creative vision.

2. **Popular AI Video Generators:**
   - **Luma AI's Dream Machine:**

o **_Overview_**: Launched in 2024, Dream Machine by Luma AI is a state-of-the-art AI video generator that has quickly gained attention for its ability to create high-quality, realistic videos from text prompts and images. It's particularly noted for its efficiency, generating up to 120 frames in just 120 seconds.

o **_Key Features_**: High-resolution output, smooth motion, and the capability to handle high traffic.

o **_Use Case_**: Ideal for creators needing quick yet detailed visual content.

- **Pika Labs**:

  o **_Overview_**: Pika Labs offers a robust platform for AI-powered video creation and editing. It's designed to be user-friendly while maintaining a high standard of production quality, making it a strong contender in the AI video generation market.

  o **_Key Features_**: Versatile editing tools, intuitive interface, and support for both simple and complex video projects.

  o **_Use Case_**: Perfect for content creators, marketers, and educators who need to produce and edit videos quickly.

- **Runway Gen-3 Alpha Turbo**:

  o **_Overview_**: Runway's Gen-3 Alpha Turbo stands out for its real-time video generation capabilities, allowing creators to produce videos almost instantly. It's a powerful tool for those who need to balance speed with high-quality output.

  o **_Key Features_**: Real-time generation, advanced video editing tools, and high-speed processing.

  o **_Use Case_**: Ideal for filmmakers, social media creators, and advertisers who need to turn around content quickly.

- **Synthesia**:

  o **_Overview_**: Synthesia is an AI video platform focused on creating videos with realistic avatars. It's widely used in corporate environments for training videos, product demonstrations, and personalized video communications.

  o **_Key Features_**: Text-to-video generation, customizable avatars, and seamless integration with business applications.

o *Use Case*: Best for businesses and creators looking to produce professional, scalable video content.

Advantages of Using AI Video Generators

AI video generators offer several advantages that can significantly enhance your animation projects:

1. **Time Efficiency**:
    *   *Faster Production*: AI tools can generate animations much faster than traditional methods, allowing you to produce more content in less time. This efficiency is particularly beneficial for creators working with tight deadlines or needing to produce high volumes of content.
    *   *Automation of Repetitive Tasks*: AI can automate tasks such as rigging, rendering, and certain aspects of character animation, freeing up your time to focus on more creative elements.

2. **Accessibility**:
    *   *Lower Skill Barriers*: AI video generators make animation accessible to a broader audience, including those without extensive technical skills. This democratization of content creation allows more people to express their creativity through animation.
    *   *User-Friendly Interfaces*: Many AI tools feature intuitive interfaces that make it easy for beginners to start creating high-quality animations.

3. **Creative Experimentation**:
    *   *Exploration of New Styles*: AI tools enable creators to explore new artistic styles and techniques that might not be feasible with manual methods. Experimenting with different AI settings can lead to unique visual effects and creative breakthroughs.
    *   *Enhanced Collaboration*: AI tools can facilitate collaboration across different skill sets, enabling, for example, a writer to generate an animated video from a script without needing a full animation team.

4. **Scalability**:

- ***High-Volume Content Creation***: AI tools are ideal for scaling content production, allowing for the creation of multiple videos or animations simultaneously. This capability is particularly useful for marketing campaigns, social media content, or educational series.
- ***Personalization***: AI allows for the creation of personalized content at scale, making it easier to tailor videos to specific audience segments or individual preferences.

Integrating AI Video Generators into Your Workflow

To maximize the potential of AI video generators, consider the following strategies for integrating them into your workflow:

1. **Start Small and Experiment**:
   - ***Begin with Simple Projects***: Start with small, manageable projects to get accustomed to how AI tools work. Experiment with different inputs, styles, and settings to understand the capabilities and limitations of the technology.
   - ***Gradually Expand Your Use***: As you become more comfortable with AI video generators, start integrating them into larger projects. Use AI to streamline specific parts of your workflow, such as character animation or background generation.

2. **Combine AI with Traditional Techniques**:
   - ***Hybrid Approach***: Use AI tools alongside traditional animation software to enhance your work. For example, you can use AI to generate basic animations and then refine them using manual techniques in software like Adobe Animate or Blender.
   - ***Fine-Tuning and Polishing***: AI-generated content often requires some level of fine-tuning to meet professional standards. Be prepared to edit and polish AI-generated animations to ensure they meet your creative vision.

3. **Consider Ethical Implications**:
   - ***Transparency***: Be transparent about the use of AI in your content creation process. This helps build trust with your audience and ensures there are no misunderstandings about the origins of your work.
   - ***Creative Integrity***: While AI can enhance creativity, it's important to ensure that the final product reflects your

unique vision. Use AI as a tool to support your creativity, not replace it.

4. **Stay Updated on AI Trends**:
   - *Continuous Learning*: AI technology is rapidly evolving, with new tools and updates being released regularly. Stay informed about the latest developments in AI video generation to keep your skills and workflow up to date.
   - *Join AI Communities*: Engage with online communities focused on AI and animation. These communities can provide valuable insights, tips, and support as you navigate the world of AI-powered content creation.

The Future of AI in Animation

As AI technology continues to advance, its impact on the animation industry is likely to grow. Here are some trends and possibilities to watch for:

1. **Increased Automation**:
   - *More Sophisticated Tools*: We can expect AI tools to become even more sophisticated, capable of handling complex tasks with minimal human intervention.
   - *Full Automation*: In the future, AI could fully automate the animation process, from concept to final production, revolutionizing content creation and enabling personalized, high-quality videos at scale.

2. **AI-Driven Creativity**:
   - *AI as a Creative Partner*: AI is evolving from being just a tool to a creative partner, helping artists brainstorm ideas, generate concepts, and collaborate on the artistic direction of projects.
   - *Generative Design*: AI could play a key role in generative design, where algorithms create unique visual patterns and animations that would be difficult for humans to conceive on their own.

3. **Ethical Considerations**:
   - *Balancing Automation with Human Creativity*: As AI becomes more capable, there will be ongoing debates about the balance between automation and human creativity. Ensuring that AI complements rather than replaces human artistry will be crucial.

- *Copyright and Ownership*: The question of who owns AI-generated content—whether it's the creator, the AI developer, or another entity—will become increasingly important as AI tools become more widespread.

By staying informed about these trends and embracing AI as a tool for innovation, you can position yourself at the forefront of the animation industry, ready to explore the new possibilities that AI brings to the creative process.

CONCLUSION

As you reach the end of this journey through creating, promoting, and monetizing animated videos, it's important to reflect on what you've learned and how to apply it moving forward. This conclusion will recap the key points covered in the book, offer tips for ongoing success, and leave you with some final words of encouragement as you continue your creative journey.

Recap of Key Points

Throughout this book, we've explored every aspect of creating animated videos and building a successful YouTube channel. Here's a quick recap of the most important points:

1. **Getting Started with Animation**: We began by understanding the basics of animation, exploring different types of animation software, and choosing the right tools based on your skills and budget. Starting with simple, beginner-friendly options helps you build confidence and develop your animation style.

2. **Planning Your Animated Video Content**: Planning is crucial to producing high-quality content. Identifying your niche, developing a content strategy, scripting, storyboarding, and designing characters and scenes all contribute to creating engaging animations that resonate with your audience.

3. **Creating and Optimizing Your YouTube Channel**: Setting up a professional YouTube channel involves creating a strong brand, designing eye-catching thumbnails and channel art, and writing effective titles and descriptions. Using SEO strategies and optimizing your content for YouTube's algorithm are key to attracting viewers and growing your channel.

4. **Uploading and Promoting Your Videos**: Effective video promotion involves cross-promotion on social media, collaborations, and engaging with your audience. Understanding how to use YouTube Studio for optimization, adding subtitles, setting up playlists, and analyzing your performance helps you maximize your

reach and impact.

5. **Monetization Strategies**: We explored various ways to monetize your channel, including ad revenue, affiliate marketing, sponsored content, selling merchandise, and crowdfunding. Diversifying your income streams helps create financial stability and supports long-term growth.

6. **Expanding Beyond YouTube**: Expanding your content to other platforms like Instagram, TikTok, and Facebook allows you to reach new audiences. Leveraging your animation skills for freelance work, creating content for brands, and building a sustainable business are key to scaling your success.

7. **Troubleshooting and Overcoming Challenges**: Every creator faces challenges, from technical issues to staying motivated. We discussed common animation mistakes, managing time and resources effectively, staying consistent, and adapting to algorithm changes. Overcoming these challenges is essential for long-term success.

Tips for Ongoing Success

As you continue your journey in animation and content creation, here are some tips to keep you on the path to success:

1. **Keep Learning**: The world of animation and digital content is constantly evolving. Stay curious and committed to learning new techniques, tools, and trends. Take online courses, attend webinars, and participate in workshops to sharpen your skills and stay ahead of the curve.

2. **Experiment and Innovate**: Don't be afraid to try new things and push the boundaries of your creativity. Experiment with different animation styles, formats, and storytelling techniques. Innovation keeps your content fresh and engaging, helping you stand out in a crowded digital landscape.

3. **Engage with Your Community**: Building a community around your content is key to sustaining long-term success. Regularly engage with your audience through comments, social media, live streams, and community posts. Listen to their feedback, respond to their questions, and involve them in your creative process.

4. **Be Consistent**: Consistency is crucial to building a loyal audience.

Stick to a regular posting schedule, maintain a consistent style, and stay true to your brand. Over time, your consistency will pay off as you build trust and recognition with your viewers.

5. **Adapt to Change**: The digital landscape is dynamic, with frequent changes in algorithms, platform policies, and viewer preferences. Stay flexible and be ready to adapt your strategies as needed. Embrace change as an opportunity to learn and grow.

6. **Balance Creativity and Business**: While it's important to focus on the creative side of animation, don't neglect the business aspects. Set financial goals, track your income and expenses, and continually look for ways to diversify your revenue streams. Balancing creativity with smart business practices is key to sustaining your career.

Final Words of Encouragement

Embarking on the journey of creating animated content and building a successful YouTube channel is both challenging and rewarding. There will be times when you face obstacles, feel overwhelmed, or question your progress. But remember that every successful creator started where you are now—taking that first step, learning through trial and error, and gradually building something meaningful.

Your passion for animation is your greatest asset. It's what will drive you to keep going, even when the path ahead seems uncertain. Trust in your creativity, stay committed to your goals, and celebrate every milestone along the way, no matter how small.

As you move forward, keep in mind that success doesn't happen overnight. It's the result of consistent effort, continuous learning, and the courage to take risks. Be patient with yourself, stay focused, and never lose sight of why you started this journey in the first place.

You have the tools, knowledge, and passion to make your mark in the world of animation. Whether you're creating content for fun, sharing your knowledge, or building a business, your unique voice and vision matter. The world is waiting to see what you create—so go out there and share your story with confidence and pride.

Thank you for taking the time to explore this guide. Now, it's time to put what you've learned into action. Keep animating, keep growing, and most importantly, keep believing in yourself. The possibilities are endless, and your journey is just beginning.

APPENDIX

The appendix provides additional resources, tools, templates, and a glossary of terms to help you as you continue your animation journey. Whether you're looking for specific tools, need a checklist to stay organized, or want to clarify some industry jargon, this section is designed to be your go-to reference.

Resource List

Tools for Animation:

1. **Adobe Animate**: A versatile 2D animation software widely used for creating interactive content and animations.

2. **Blender**: A free, open-source 3D animation software with powerful features for modeling, texturing, and rendering.

3. **Toon Boom Harmony**: Industry-standard software for 2D animation, used in TV and film production.

4. **Animaker**: A web-based tool for creating simple, drag-and-drop animations.

5. **Canva**: A design tool that includes basic animation features, ideal for creating animated social media posts.

6. **Doodly**: Software for creating whiteboard animation videos.

7. **Moho (Anime Studio)**: 2D animation software with a focus on character animation and rigging.

Video Editing Tools:

1. **Adobe Premiere Pro**: Industry-standard video editing software.

2. **DaVinci Resolve**: Professional video editing and color correction software, available in both free and paid versions.

3.   **iMovie**: A beginner-friendly video editing software for Mac users.

Sound and Music Resources:

1. **Audacity**: Free, open-source audio editing software.

2. **Epidemic Sound**: A music library offering royalty-free tracks for content creators.

3. **Freesound**: A collaborative database of Creative Commons licensed sound effects.

Online Tutorials and Courses:

1. **Skillshare**: Offers a variety of courses on animation, video editing, and content creation.

2. **Udemy**: An online learning platform with courses on animation, video production, and more.

3. **YouTube Creators Academy**: Free resources and courses from YouTube to help you grow your channel.

Communities and Forums

1. **Reddit – r/animation**: A community of animators sharing advice, feedback, and resources.

2. **Animation Mentor Community**: A forum for students and professionals in the animation industry.

3. **Discord Animation Communities**: Various Discord servers where animators can connect, collaborate, and share their work.

Templates and Checklists

Project Planning Checklist:
o   Define your video's purpose and target audience.
o   Develop a content strategy.
o   Write a script and create a storyboard.
o   Design characters and backgrounds.
o   Plan your production schedule with specific deadlines.

- o Gather resources (music, sound effects, software tools).
- o Set up your workspace and tools.
- o Review the script and storyboard for any changes before starting animation.

YouTube Video Upload Checklist:
- Create a compelling title with relevant keywords.
- Write a detailed description with links and a call-to-action.
- Design and upload a custom thumbnail.
- Add appropriate tags and keywords.
- Enable monetization and set ad preferences (if applicable).
- Set the video's visibility (Public, Unlisted, or Private).
- Add subtitles or closed captions.
- Create an end screen and add cards for additional content.
- Double-check all settings before publishing.

Collaboration and Sponsorship Checklist:
- Identify potential collaborators or sponsors that align with your content.
- Prepare a proposal or pitch that outlines the benefits of working together.
- Clarify the terms of collaboration, including deliverables, deadlines, and compensation.
- Create a contract or agreement to formalize the partnership.
- Maintain regular communication throughout the collaboration.
- Review the final product together and make necessary revisions.
- Promote the collaboration across all relevant platforms.

Glossary of Terms
- **Ad Revenue**: Income generated from ads placed on your YouTube videos through the YouTube Partner Program.
- **Algorithm**: The set of rules used by platforms like YouTube to determine which content is shown to users.
- **Animation**: The process of creating the illusion of movement by displaying a series of images or frames in rapid succession.
- **Aspect Ratio**: The width-to-height ratio of a video screen, with common ratios being 16:9 for widescreen and 1:1 for square videos.
- **Bumper Ad**: A short, non-skippable ad that plays before, during, or after a YouTube video.
- **CPM (Cost Per Thousand Impressions)**: A metric used to calculate ad revenue based on the number of times an ad is shown per thousand views.
- **Freelancing**: Working independently to provide services, such as animation or video production, to clients on a contract basis.

- **Keyframe**: A specific point in the animation timeline where a change occurs, such as a character's position or shape.

Monetization: The process of earning money from your content, typically through ads, sponsorships, or product sales.

- **Patreon**: A membership platform that allows creators to receive monthly support from fans in exchange for exclusive content or perks.
- **SEO (Search Engine Optimization)**: The practice of optimizing content to rank higher in search engine results, making it easier for people to find your videos.
- **Storyboard**: A visual plan or sequence of drawings that outlines the scenes and actions in a video before it is animated or filmed.
- **Thumbnails**: The preview image for a video, which viewers see before clicking to watch. A well-designed thumbnail can increase click-through rates.
- **Watch Time**: The total amount of time viewers spend watching your videos, a key metric for YouTube's algorithm.

This appendix provides you with the resources, tools, templates, and terminology you need to navigate the world of animation and content creation confidently. Whether you're just starting or looking to refine your skills, this section is designed to support you at every stage of your journey.

www.ingramcontent.com/pod-product-compliance
Lightning Source LLC
Chambersburg PA
CBHW071553080326
40690CB00056B/1815